HONEY FOR YOU HONEY FOR ME

A First Book of Nursery Rhymes

illustrated by

Chris Riddell

collected by

Michael Rosen

ABOUT THIS BOOK

Whenever I visit schools, I listen out on the playground for old rhymes being shared and new rhymes being invented. I can remember learning them in this way when I was a boy – passing them on, and keeping them alive, by word of mouth.

Nursery rhymes are wonderful and surprising little dramas, full of mysteries and unanswered questions. They help us to engage with the world around us, in all its strangeness and richness, from a very young age. And when you begin gathering this great body together, it becomes an unofficial record of our culture – and tells us a good deal about our hopes, desires, fears and failings.

I have collected books of nursery rhymes for many years. For centuries, people have been

publishing folk songs, children's lullabies and ditties in anthologies. Looking through some of these old collections, I found a few intriguing gems which I feel have been neglected.

For this new book, I've placed those rhymes beside some that you may already know and love. They're full of jokes and unsolved riddles, which are interesting to think about and perfect for sharing. On that note, it's worth putting a moment's thought into how to use this collection.

It goes without saying that the simplest way is the best: sit with a child, read the rhymes out loud together and look at Chris Riddell's wonderful pictures. But it can also help to sing the words or make up actions, to show how sounds, rhythm and emotion can be conveyed through the whole body.

We're not statues and we don't stand still, and the same is true of our language: it reflects what we borrow and what we invent. Old and new, these rhymes are perfect proof.

MICHAEL ROSEN

Engine, engine, number nine

Going down Chicago line.

If the train goes off the track,

Do you want your money back?

Yes? No? Maybe so!

From **Wibbleton** to **Wobbleton** is fifteen miles,

From **Wobbleton** to **Wibbleton** is fifteen miles,

From **Wibbleton** to **Wobbleton**,

From **Wobbleton** to **Wibbleton**,

From **Wibbleton** to **Wobbleton** is fifteen miles.

11

Leg over leg,
As the dog went to Dover.
When he came to a stile,

JUMP!

TO DOVER →

He went over.

To market, to market,

To buy a plum bun.

Home again, home again,

Market is done.

Dibbity, dibbity, dibbity, doe,

Give me a pancake and I'll go.

Dibbity, dibbity, dibbity, ditter,

Please to give me a bit of a fritter.

Bat, bat, come under my hat,
And I'll give you a slice of bacon;
And when I bake, I'll give you a cake,
If I am not mistaken.

Little Poll Parrot

Sat in his garret

Eating toast and tea.

A little brown mouse

Jumped into the house

And stole it all away.

"C R O A K !"

said the toad. "I'm hungry, I think;

Today I've had nothing to eat or to drink.

I'll crawl to a garden and jump through the rails,

And there I'll dine nicely on slugs and on snails."

Hickup-snickup,

Stand up, straight up;

One drop, two drops,

Good for the hiccup.

One, two,

Mary's at the

Five, six,

Eating cherries

Ippy dippy dation,

My operation,

How many buses

At the station?

CLAP, CLAP, CLAP!

Miss Mary Mack Mack Mack

All dressed in **black black black**,

With silver buttons buttons buttons

All down her back back back.

She asked her mother mother mother

For fifty **cents cents cents**

To see the elephants elephants elephants

Jump over the fence fence fence.

They jumped so high high high

They reached the **sky sky sky**.

They didn't come back back back

Till the Fourth of July July July!

Polly, Dolly, Kate and Molly,

All are filled with pride and folly.

Polly tattles; Dolly wriggles;

Katy rattles; Molly giggles.

Whoever knew such constant rattling,

Wriggling, giggling, noise and tattling?

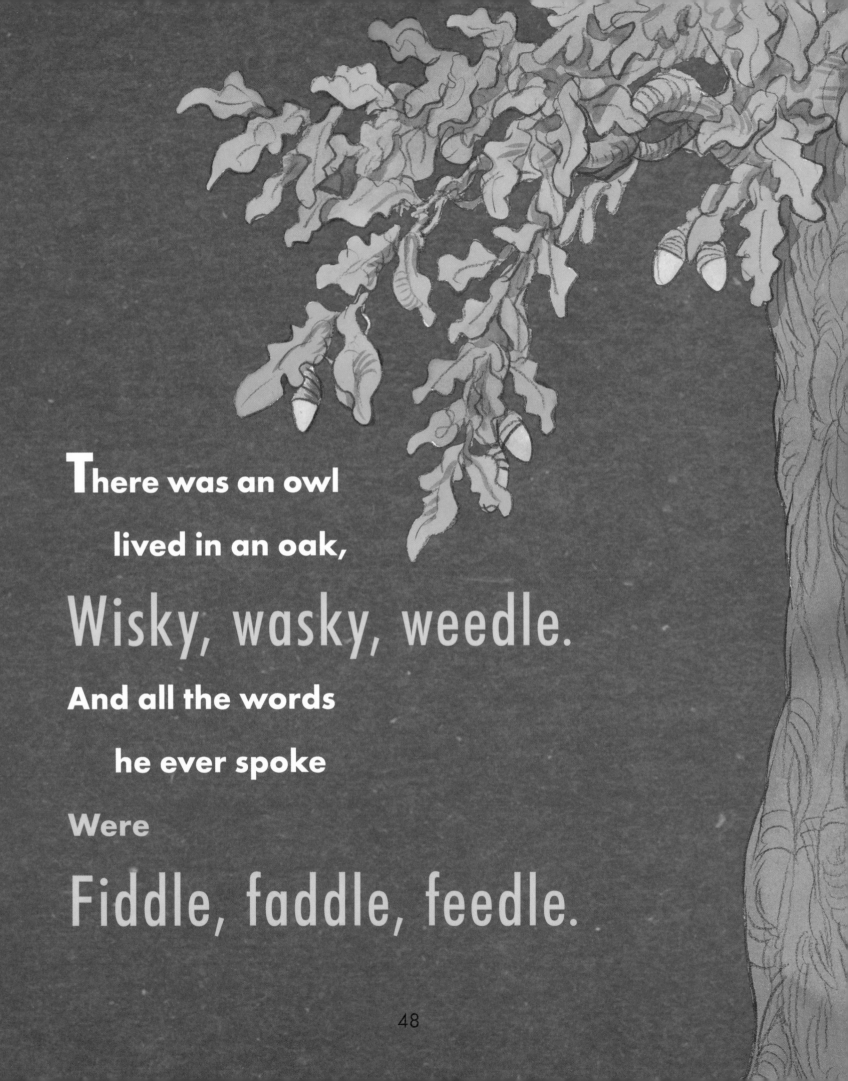

There was an owl
lived in an oak,

Wisky, wasky, weedle.

And all the words
he ever spoke

Were

Fiddle, faddle, feedle.

The man in the wilderness said to me,

"How many strawberries

grow in the sea?"

I answered him, as I thought good,

"As many red herrings as

grow in the wood."

Hab can nab

The two-pound crab,

The tuppenny ha'penny lobster,

Trot over to France

To see the cat dance,

And couldn't come

back to his master.

53

Dickory, dickory, dare,

The pig flew up in the air.

The man in brown

Soon brought him down,

Dickory, dickory, dare.

Higgledy, piggledy, **pop**!

The dog has eaten the **mop**.

The pig's in a **hurry**,

The cat's in a **flurry**,

Higgledy, piggledy, **pop**!

One, two, three,

Mother finds a flea,

Puts it in the teapot

And makes a cup of tea.

The flea jumps out,

Mother gives a shout,

And down comes Father

With his shirt hanging out.

Four, five, six,

Father's in a fix,

Wants to get the billy goat

And hatch a few more chicks.

The chicks hatch out,

Father gives a shout,

And down comes Granny

With her hair sticking out.

Seven, eight, nine,

Granny's doing fine,

Scrubs all the children

And pegs them on the line.

The line gives way,

Granny shouts, "Hey!"

"Wow!" cry the children

And they all run away.

Once I saw a little bird
Come *hop, hop, hop,*
So I cried, **"Little bird,**

Will you stop, stop, stop?"

I was going to the window
To say **"How do you do?"**
But he shook his little tail
And a w a y h e f l e w.

The north wind doth blow,

And we shall have snow,

And what will poor Robin do then?

Poor thing!

He'll sit in a barn

And keep himself warm

And hide his head under his wing.

Poor thing!

April showers bring May flowers.

Rain on the green grass,

Rain on the tree,

Rain on the housetop,

But not on **ME**.

This is the key of the kingdom.

In that kingdom there is a city.

In that city there is a town.

In that town there is a street.

In that street there is a lane.

In that lane there is a yard.

In that yard there is a house.

In that house there is a room.

In that room there is a bed.

On that bed there is a basket.

In that basket there are some flowers.

Flowers in the basket;

Basket on the bed;

Bed in the room;

Room in the house;

House in the yard;

Yard in the lane;

Lane in the street;

Street in the town;

Town in the city;

City in the kingdom.

This is the key of the kingdom.

He who would see old Hoghton right
Must view it by the pale moonlight.

The man in the moon

Came down too soon,

And asked his way to Norwich.

He went by the south

And burnt his mouth

With supping cold plum porridge.

Diddle, diddle, dumpling,

my son John,

Went to bed with his trousers on;

One shoe off, and one shoe on,

Diddle, diddle, dumpling,

my son John.

Who wants breakfast?

Who wants tea?

Who wants everything

Just like me?

Honey for breakfast,

Honey for tea.

Honey for YOU,

Honey for ME.

Tom could not, WOULD not leave.

"**NO!**" he shouted.

But his angry words floated over Dad's head, away, away, like soundless bubbles.

Tom had to do something.
He went out on his triple-extender trolley-bike,

thinking, thinking, thinking . . .

. . . then, faster than a falling leaf, he had an idea.

It was BIGGER than autumn
– a brilliant, hope-filled, **HUGE** idea!

He rushed home to share it with Dad.

But Dad just murmured,

"Hmmm, that's nice."

So Tom tried again.

And again.

"You see?! We can open our house to visitors so everyone can see our amazing inventions. We can call it

The Museum of Vehicles Made From Things Not Usually Used For Making Vehicles!"

"You know what," said Dad, after what felt like hours. "That's not a bad idea, Tom!"

And he smiled for the first time in eleven sunsets. That month, their home buzzed, busy with excitement.

Together Tom and Dad
tested and fixed,

scrubbed, oiled and painted

and polished until their vehicles
glittered blink-bright.

Nothing, nothing like this
had ever been seen,

or even IMAGINED!

Visitors came from near and far. They gaped at the miniature banana-powered rocket.

They gasped at the ingenious Mappolator.

They gawped at the piano airship.

They stared at the tandem bathicoptor,

the mechanical hummingbird,

the remote-control submarine.

All around the museum were sighs of wonder and laughter like sunlight.

They giggled at the moustachicoptor zig-zagging wonkily.
They chuckled at the high-powered, self-flushing, superspeed-system toilet racer.

Visitors poured in from near and even more far
and, after a few weeks . . .

. . . Dad announced they could stay in their house.

Their home.

But then one cold night, a whirlwind skittled through
the dark, sucking up all things and spitting them far.

Their home was now mostly rubble,
just a few strewn bits of broken exhibits
poking skywards in the white snowfields.

Why can't good things ever stay the way they are? thought Tom.

"We can rebuild it!" said Dad brightly, full of badly-hidden sad.

But Tom said, "It could happen again.
The weather is as unpredictable as dreams."
Tom couldn't stand it.

Why, why, **WHY?!**

He tried riding and thinking again,
but his head felt as empty as that sky.

When he arrived home,
Dad was grinning wildly.
He'd had a really, really BIG idea.
"We'll rebuild our home into an amazing,

MOVING museum!"

"Dad," said Tom proudly, grinning wider than summer, "you're a genius. A complete GENIUS!"

That month they oiled, painted, polished, fixed, scrubbed and cleaned.

And soon their mobile museum-home could

walk,

float,

gallop

and even . . .

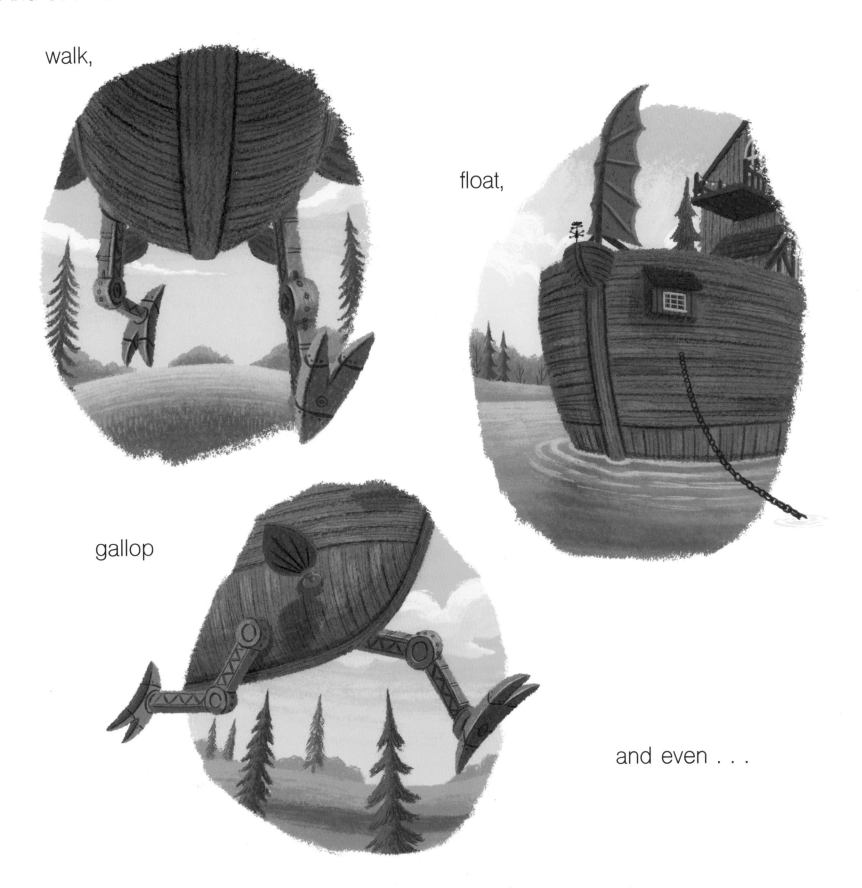

. . . FLY!

And each evening, after museum closing time,
Tom and his dad would surf the skies,

whooping-happy and racing shooting stars.